when High Priests Take Over the Nursery

when HIGH PRIESTS TAKE OVER THE NURSERY

BY JON CLARK

CFI
An imprint of Cedar Fort, Inc.
Springville, Utah

This is a work of fiction. The characters, names, incidents, places, and dialogue are products of the author's imagination and are not to be construed as real. The views expressed within this work are the sole responsibility of the author and do not necessarily reflect the position of Cedar Fort, Inc., or any other entity.

ISBN 13: 978-1-59955-977-3

Published by CFI, an imprint of Cedar Fort, Inc.
2373 W. 700 S., Springville, UT, 84663
Distributed by Cedar Fort, Inc., www.cedarfort.com

Cover design by Danie Romrell
Cover design © 2012 by Lyle Mortimer
Edited and typeset by Kelley Konzak

Printed in the United States of America

10 9 8 7 6 5 4 3 2 1

Printed on acid-free paper

Today, after APC, there will be BYC. Tomorrow, for the YSA there will be an FHE. The guest speaker is an RM from BYU who will speak about the 14th AoF: We believe in acronyms...

CLARK

Jon Clark

Bishop, I finally got an appointment for an interview with that inactivey guy... Bad news is it's for the 35th of the month.
CLARK

I want to add my testimony to those already given...and subtract it from all the extensive travelogues and unnecessary gibberish.
CLARK

Jon Clark

OK, are we all clear on what we're going to forget to do?
WARD COUNCIL
CLARK

The bishop is concerned about iPod games during sacrament meeting...
CLARK

Jon Clark

Ant Church

To check you for ADD, we monitored your attention levels during conference talks...
ATTENTION LEVEL
10
0
ANECDOTE/JOKES
BODY OF TALK
AMEN
CLARK

Son, don't get me wrong, I appreciate your unwavering righteousness...But you're a bishop's kid...For heaven's sake act like one!
CLARK

Clark
You have reached the bishop's office. If you need to confess, press 1. For all other needs, complaints, and concerns, please hang up and call the elders quorum president.

Jon Clark

We'd like to call Brother Wilburn to be the new Young Womens president...Dagnabit, I botched that-it's Brother Wellborne.
CLARK

Well, well...I see a lot of new faces here today, brothers and sisters. Indeed, the Botox industry is alive and well in our ward...

CLARK

My name is Brother Retention. I just felt like I needed to come up here. But what do I know? I'm just the elephant in this half-empty chapel...
CLARK

Jon Clark

CLARK
So you feel a little burned out in your calling, Sister Jorgensen?

And now, after his twenty years of faithful service, we'd like to release Brother Williams as the stake clerk... but we can't.
CLARK

...And after listening to conference, I know that C.S. Lewis was a true prophet of God...
CLARK

Before we begin this single adult conference,
I have some exciting news to announce...
Marie Osmond is single again!
CLARK

Jon Clark

Brothers and sisters, the bishop has just sent a note to me that says,"HOLD STILL!"
CLARK

Church just got a whole lot better once Brother Griggs found the recliner handle on his pew...
Clark

Jon Clark

We appreciate all those who participated in last night's church dance...I, for one, am still stuck in a disco move...
CLARK

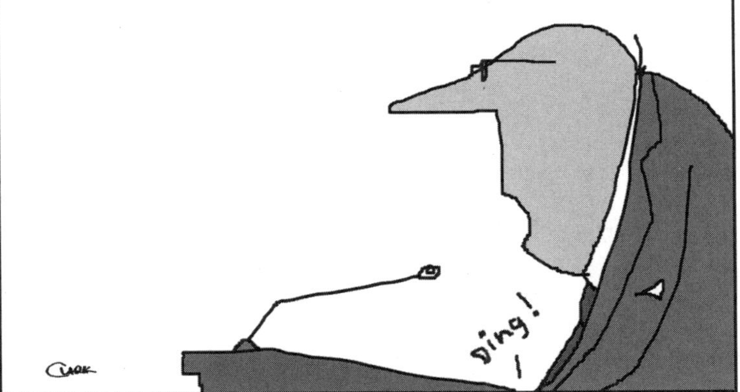
Brothers and sisters, the time is now yours for the bearing of testimonies. Please note that due to ward budget shortfalls, we've installed a coin slot up here on the podium. A quarter will keep the mic on for one minute...so feel free to take all the time you need.
Ding!

Jon Clark

I assure you this interview is completely confidential...
CLARK
BISHOP

Worshipping is like driving—it requires <u>conscious</u> effort...

Jon Clark

CLARK
You seem a bit defensive about my counsel, Brother Hancock...

I haven't had to speak in church since 1963, when I gave a talk titled "The Colorful Teachings of J. Golden Kimball."
CLARK

Jon Clark

Brethren, the sisters say they are tired of cleaning up our messes and getting everything done in the ward...So, how do we get them to see the blessings in it?

PEC

We forgot the sacrament bread, Bishop...
But don't worry, the donut shop is open
on fast Sunday.

Jon Clark

Sister Franks, we'd like to call you as the new Relief Society president... And if you start today, I'll arrange to have your pay doubled...
CLARK

Brethren, if we're gonna do these early-morning bishopric meetings, by golly, we're gonna do 'em right! Brother Tanner, how do you like your eggs?
CLARK

Jon Clark

It's an echo chamber in case, as a bishop, I need to call someone to repentance.

DO YOUR HOME TEACHING!
Must be the end of the month...

Why am I up here?...Because the gospel is true, brothers and sisters, even on bad hair days.
CLARK

This report is exceptional, Brother Jones. Indeed, you are a marvelous clerk and a wonder.
CLARK
CLARK

Jon Clark

...And I want to express my love to my very supportive and exemplary family. Son, please put down the laser pointer...

HAPPY FATHER'S DAY!

Jon Clark

I've purchased enough fireworks for you to light under each of your auxiliary and quorum members... Now if that doesn't get them to do something, brothers and sisters, I don't know what will.

Brother Grant's first time speaking...

What would happen in a bishopric meeting if hell ever froze.

Food storage saved us, brothers and sisters...If it wasn't for our homeowners storing wheat in their basement, we'd all be dead by now.

Jon Clark

While I certainly appreciate the foresight, Sister Dingley, a sign-up sheet for refreshments for the Second Coming is a bit premature...
CLARK

Hi, I'm Bishop Rollins. Are you two fresh meat in the ward or just visiting?
CLARK

Jon Clark

Brothers and sisters, I had a gambling addiction. Then, the bishop bet me that I couldn't quit. Now I'm cured, and I won fifty bucks!

CLARK

Games we play in Sunday School...

Jon Clark

Leaving so soon? Don't you know that church is three hours long so we can get used to eternity?
CLARK

How am I doing on time, Bishop?
86
108
21

Jon Clark

...We pray for those who have prepared inspired messages for us...and especially for those who haven't...
Clark

Jon Clark

Bishop, I think Jimmermania is getting out of hand. The Primary children are singing, "I hope they call me on a mission, unless I have grown a foot or two..."
JIMMER FREDETTE
CLARK

Those were inspired messages we just heard...I'm sure we have all clicked "like" in our hearts.

Jon Clark

We have some lost and found items that may belong to someone in a stressful calling. Let's see, there's patience, a temper, sanity...
CLARK

As we older members pass on, I would encourage you young married couples to multiply and replenish the ward.
CLARK

Jon Clark

One way to get members to not sit in the same row every sacrament meeting...

You were right about the Lord working in mysterious ways, Brother Grant...Not five minutes into your talk and my insomnia was flat cured.
CLARK

Jon Clark

...And what I really like about our ward
is that we never judge each other.
5.9

No, I'm not too old for a calling, Bishop...as long as I don't have to see anything, hear anything, or be away from the toilet for too long...

Not-So-High Councilor...

...And any opposed to Brother Rigby being called as your tireless, never-home bishop, please signify by the same sign...One hand is sufficient, Sister Rigby.
CLARK

Jon Clark

CLARK
Brother Cox, if you're going to be the executive secretary, you've got to get the interview schedule right. I just interviewed a cheating husband for baptism and disfellowshipped an eight-year-old kid!

Unfortunately, my kids aren't here today...One little piggy went to the market, and the other little piggy stayed home.
CLARK

Pig Church

Jon Clark

You've done an excellent job of playing dead in the ward, Brother Fido...but now we'd like to ask you to speak.

CLARK

I call it the PLEASY BUTTON, Bishop...Just one click and you can please the entire ward!
CLARK

Jon Clark

Our Primary program is titled
"I can learn to follow Him,
when I take my Ritalin."
FOLLOW

Rabbit Church

Jon Clark

CLARK
You say you never see your husband because of his church calling... Remind me who he is again...
You, Bishop...

The Church stays out of presidential politics, brothers and sisters...Each of us must decide for ourselves whether to vote for Romney or Huntsman...
CLARK

Jon Clark

"If ye love me, keep money in my bank account."

When High Priests Take Over the Nursery

Jon Clark

Saturday

Brother Barker, as the new elders quorum president, you will have countless opportunities for service... So if you have a pickup truck, sell it fast.

CLARK

Jon Clark

Priesthood Session

Brothers and sisters, we want to subtly remind you that this is a three-hour block of meetings.
LEGO
CLARK

...Late that Sunday night, Sister Fleming suddenly remembered what she had left at church...
Z z z z
CLARK

Well, single adults, I have good news and bad news: The good news is that if we are righteous, we will all one day have an eternal companion...The bad news is that it won't be Marie Osmond, since she just remarried again...

Brother Tipton, just because you are in a huge BYU singles ward doesn't mean we can't find a meaningful calling for you... In fact, we are in desperate need of a ward doorstop tracker.

It's OK, sweetie, I promise you won't get skin cancer from being a Sunbeam.
RM207
SUNBEAMS
CLARK

Jon Clark

I'm not sure how you see me, brothers and sisters, but we bishops are not super-humans.
CLARK

...So if you don't want to be gonged–testimonies only!
CLARK

Jon Clark

We'd like to thank those who bore testimonies up here today...And to those who bore testimonies in their hearts, we say: Don't wuss out next time...
CLARK

I have so many blessings from the Lord I can't count them all. But I'm going to try: Number one...
CLARK

Jon Clark

If any of you are thinking of leaving ward council early, let me remind you that "we are all enlisted till the conflict is o'er..."
CLARK

CLARK
Brother Williams and I both pay half our tithing...So we were wondering if we could get a sort of time-share temple recommend.

Jon Clark

We need to be more united as a bishopric...Any ideas, Brother Freedman?...

We'd like to have more unity and hope among the older single sisters in the ward. So we were wondering, Bishop, if you would marry all of us in the hereafter...
CLARK

Jon Clark

I know the resurrection is free...
but what are the upgrades
gonna cost me?
CLARK

We are deeply concerned about members who have gone inactive for unknown reasons. Brother Gibbs, we'd like to call you to head up our new "What the Heck Happened to You" committee.

Jon Clark

CLARK
Well, let me tell you, young man...When I was a deacon, we had to pass the sacrament uphill down the aisle, both ways, in the snow...

...And now my life's a mess, Bishop, because I don't like my job and... Hey, what's that?
World's smallest violin...

Jon Clark

...The walls were white and padded, I was in a straitjacket, and doctors kept shoving medicine down my throat. That's when it hit me: I'm in the wrong ward!

CLARK

Do you know what zero percent home teaching means, President Huff? It means things haven't gotten any worse than the previous month, and, by golly, in this bishop's book, that's progress!

But I don't need to pay tithing, Bishop. I only make nine-tenths of an income.

CLEARANCE
SINGLE ADULTS
Kiss Kiss

About the Author

Jon Clark is a published children's book author, a cartoonist, and a music composer for TV by profession. His children's book *Anna Hosanna: The Fastest Prayer-Sayer Ever!* was published in 2007 under his pen name, J. D. Clark. He went on to self-publish five more books in the Anna Hosanna series. Jon began *Honest Jon* as an editorial cartoon for local newspapers several years prior. His cartoons have appeared in *The Mormon Times*, *The New Era*, *Sunstone*, *Highlights*, *Meridian Magazine*, and other magazines and websites. He has also created several greeting cards that sell in LDS bookstores across the country. *Honest Jon* is now a popular LDS cartoon-panel blog, http://honestjoncomics.blogspot.com. He was recently interviewed on the Mormon Channel radio program *Everything Creative* along with Brian Crane (*Pickles*) and Arie Van De Graaff. (Listen to the discussion at http://mormonchannel.org/programs/everything-creative-discussion-46?lang=eng.) He lives in Knoxville, Tennessee, with his wife and four children and serves as the executive secretary in his ward.